Journal Deep Carrot Orange Color Simple Plain Orange

(Notebook · Diary · Blank Book)

Distinctive Journals

This Book Belongs To

_____

www.DistinctiveJournals.com

© 2017 Distinctive Journals

All rights reserved.
No part of this book may be reproduced in any form or by any electronic or mechanical means, including information storage and retrieval systems, without written permission from the publisher.

Thank you for your purchase!

We hope you enjoyed your journal.

Distinctive Journals creates blank books for use as journals, diaries, and notebooks. Cover designs include stunning photographs and artwork, faux textures, simple sketches, personalized monograms and trendy patterns.

Access the entire line at:
www.DistinctiveJournals.com

Made in the USA
Monee, IL
08 December 2021